The Ultimate Co
for Runners

Delicious Recipes for Optimal Performance and Endurance - Perfect for Marathon and Ultra Runners - One-Stop Kitchen Companion for a Stronger, Faster, and Healthier You

Nick Hancock

© **Copyright 2023 by Nick Hancock. All rights reserved.**

The content contained within this book may not be reproduced, duplicated, or transmitted without direct written permission from the author or the publisher.

Under no circumstances will any blame or legal responsibility be held against the publisher, or author, for any damages, reparation, or monetary loss due to the information contained within this book. Either directly or indirectly. You are responsible for your own choices, actions, and results.

Legal Notice:

This book is copyright protected. This book is only for personal use. You cannot amend, distribute, sell, use, quote or paraphrase any part, or the content within this book, without the consent of the author or publisher.

Disclaimer Notice:

Please note the information contained within this document is for educational and entertainment purposes only. All effort has been executed to present accurate, up to date, and reliable, complete information. No warranties of any kind are declared or implied. Readers acknowledge that the author is not engaging in the rendering of legal, financial, medical or professional advice. The content within this book has been derived from various sources. Please consult a licensed professional before attempting any techniques outlined in this book. By reading this document, the reader agrees that under no circumstances is the author responsible for any losses, direct or indirect, which are incurred as a result of the use of the information contained within this document, including, but not limited to, — errors, omissions, or inaccuracies.

Table of Contents

Chapter 1: Understanding Nutrients 1

    The three macronutrients 1

    The role of each macronutrient in fueling your runs and aiding in recovery 3

    Carb Loading for Marathons and Ultramarathons 4

        What Is Carb Loading? 4

        Why Is Carb Loading for Runners Important? 4

        How to Carb Load for a Marathon or Ultra Run 4

        Foods To Eat When Carbohydrate Loading 5

        Stay Fuelled on Race Day 5

    The importance of hydration for running performance 6

Chapter 2: Eating for Energy 7

    The best foods to eat before and after runs 7

    Tips for fueling during long runs and races 8

    Nutrition For Long-Distance Runners 9

Chapter 3: Meal Planning and Grocery Shopping 13

    How to plan your meals for the week 13

Chapter 4: Frequently Asked Questions and Troubleshooting 14

    Common questions about nutrition and running performance 14

    How to adjust your diet for injuries or illnesses 16

Chapter 5 Breakfast 18

    Biscoff Porridge 19

    Oat and blueberry pancakes 21

    Bagel with smoked Salmon and cucumber 23

    Peanut butter overnight oats with strawberries and blueberries 24

Scrambled egg and Avo on toast! — 26

Biscoff Breakfast cheesecake — 28

Protein pancakes with nut butter and banana — 30

Dark chocolate overnight oats — 32

Veggie Breakfast "Fry Up" — 34

Cinnamon and raisin bagel with PB, Jam and banana — 36

Chapter 6 Lunch — 37

Smokey BBQ Chicken Nachos — 38

Tuna pasta salad with tomato, peppers and olives — 40

Crispy herby chicken and mango wrap — 42

Omelette with veggies — 44

Lunchtime Raw Mega Salad — 46

Chicken & Avocado pasta salad — 48

Salmon, little trees, feta, and pasta — 50

Chicken fajita wrap with quick guacamole — 52

Japanese Poke bowl with Salmon — 54

Chapter 7 Snacks — 56

Beetroot Hummus — 57

Energy Balls! — 59

Salted Chocolate Fudge Flapjack! — 61

Banging Banana Bread! — 63

Runners Trail Mix — 65

Protein powered cheese toastie! — 66

Skyr with fruit — 67

Chapter 8 Smoothies and Bowls — 69

- Blueberry and peanut butter smoothie — 70
- Berry Fro-Yo! — 71
- Berry "Power" bowl — 72
- Super smooth fruit and nut bowl — 74
- Choconana smoothie!! — 75
- Super smoothie — 76
- Berry smoothie with chocolate — 78

Chapter 9 Dinner — 79

- Butter chicken with rice and naan — 80
- Lasagne — 82
- Peri Peri chicken and zingy rice — 84
- King prawn soft tacos — 86
- Beef Panang Curry — 88
- Teriyaki Chicken stir fry with soba noodles — 90
- Ramen bowl with chicken — 92
- Beetroot Pesto Pasta — 94
- Indian Red Lentil and Cauliflower Dal — 96
- Butternut Squash and Bean Bowl — 98
- Sweet Potato and Chickpea Salad — 100
- Beef-troot Salad! — 102
- Conclusion — 104
- Afterthought — 105

Introduction

Hey there, fellow runners! It's Nick Hancock, your friendly neighbourhood UESCA and UK Athletics Qualified Running Coach. I'm thrilled to introduce my latest book, jam-packed with 47 delicious recipes from my previous life working in hospitality has helped inspire and that I have used to fuel my running... Now I want to share them with you!

You know what's one of the most common questions I get asked by runners? What to eat! And I get it. Food is fuel, but, in my mind, it mustn't be bland or confusing. And that's why I've written this book, to make your life easier, to help you fuel your runs, and to take the guesswork out of what to eat.

As a highly experienced hospitality professional with over two decades of industry knowledge and expertise, I have managed and operated some of the most prestigious restaurants globally. My career has seen me work with respected names such as Fairmont Hotels in Singapore, luxury restaurants in Dubai, and several renowned fresh-food high-street restaurants led by legends such as Jamie Oliver, Gennaro Contaldo, and Bill Collison.

Combining my passion for great food and my love of running, I have developed 47 delicious recipes to fuel my runs. While I am not a qualified nutritionist or dietician, I have personally tested and perfected each recipe to eat delicious food while enhancing my running performance. And the results speak for themselves.

I am proud to have achieved personal records that include a 5km time of 17:28, a 10km time of 36:58, a half marathon time of 1:17:20, a marathon time of 2:53.01, and a 50km time of 3:59.04. In addition, I have earned multiple podium appearances and top-10 finishes at all distances, with particular strength at ultramarathon distances.

My running achievements include being the 1st place winner of the Maverick Adidas Terrex Jurassic Coast long course in October 2022, a 2nd place finish in May 2021 at the BigWayAround 50 km, and a 4th place finish at Brecon2Cardiff in a field of over 500 runners in one of the worst storms Britain has ever seen.

While my recipes have been developed with my performance in mind, they are packed with nutrient-rich ingredients that can benefit runners of all levels. So, whether you're a seasoned marathoner or just starting your running journey, I invite you to try my recipes and taste the difference.

As a dedicated runner and leading UK running coach, I am passionate about helping athletes achieve their performance goals. Whether you're training for a half marathon, marathon, or ultramarathon or simply looking to improve your running performance, this book will provide you with the so delicious recipes that will help fuel those runs!

In the first part of this book, we'll explore the science behind nutrition and running performance. You'll learn about the importance of macronutrients, hydration, recovery, and food's role in preventing injuries and illnesses. And in the second part, we'll dive into the 47 recipes I have carefully crafted to help you fuel your runs and support your training.

From tasty smoothies to post-run recovery snacks, these recipes are simple, easy to prepare, and use common ingredients that you can find at any local grocery store. Whether you're a novice in the kitchen or an experienced cook, you'll find these recipes quick and easy to prepare.

But this book is not just about recipes. It's about empowering you to take control of your diet and make informed decisions about what you eat. You'll learn how to plan your meals and snacks to support your training goals and make healthy choices when eating out or on the go.

And for those needing additional support, I offer coaching services to help take your training to the next level.

In addition to the recipes and tips, this book includes a troubleshooting section to address common questions and concerns about nutrition and running performance.

I'm passionate about helping athletes achieve their performance goals, and I'm excited to share my knowledge and expertise with you in this book. So whether you're a seasoned runner or a beginner looking to fuel your first 5K, this book has something for you.

So grab a copy, fuel those runs, and let's achieve your performance goals together. And don't forget to check out my website at www.maximummileagecoaching.com for additional information and coaching services.

Let's do this!

Nick

Chapter 1: Understanding Nutrients

The three macronutrients

As a running coach, I always emphasise to my clients that proper nutrition is key to performing at their best, both on and off the road and trail. One of the most fundamental aspects of nutrition is understanding the three macronutrients: carbohydrates, protein, and fat.

1: Carbohydrates

Carbohydrates are the primary source of energy for endurance athletes like runners. They are the body's preferred fuel source; therefore, it's crucial to have a sufficient intake of carbohydrates before and during runs to sustain energy levels and prevent fatigue. Foods high in carbohydrates include whole grains, fruits, vegetables, and legumes.

2: Protein

Protein is vital for muscle repair and growth, making it essential for runners looking to recover faster and build lean muscle. While carbohydrates are the primary energy source, protein is essential for repairing damage during runs and training sessions.

3: Fat

Fat is also a critical macronutrient, providing the body with energy during long runs and absorbing fat-soluble vitamins. Good sources of healthy fats include avocados, nuts, seeds, olive oil, and fatty fish. It's important to note that while fat is necessary for a nutritious diet, it's important to moderate intake to avoid consuming excessive calories.

It's crucial to balance the intake of all three macronutrients to achieve optimal performance. The amount of each macronutrient you need will vary depending on your training goals, body composition, and the duration and intensity of your runs.

As a running coach, I often see runners not getting enough carbohydrates, especially during their training runs, leading to decreased energy levels and poor performance. It is vital to fuel our runs!

To calculate your macronutrient needs, it's essential to consult a registered dietitian or use an online calculator that takes into account your individual needs and goals.

The general rule of thumb I use is a macronutrient balance consisting of around 50% carbohydrates, 30% protein, and 20% fat. This carbohydrate mix fuels my running and strength work; the protein ensures I keep my musculature and feel fuller for longer, and the fats are enough for my dietary needs and key functions in the body.

It's also important to note that the quality of the macronutrients you consume is just as important as the quantity. Opt for whole foods like fruits, vegetables, whole grains, lean proteins, and healthy fats to get the nutrients your body needs to perform at its best.

Equally, life is about balance, and some recipes will include some ingredients that I enjoy in moderation... biscoff anyone?

In conclusion, as a runner, it's essential to understand each macronutrient's role in fueling your runs and aiding in recovery. Proper balance and moderation of carbohydrates, protein, and fat are key to optimal performance. Consult a professional or use online resources to determine your macronutrient and dietary needs.

The role of each macronutrient in fueling your runs and aiding in recovery

The three macronutrients - carbohydrates, protein, and fat - are crucial in fueling your runs and aiding recovery. Each macronutrient serves a unique purpose in the body and should be adequately consumed to optimise your performance.

Carbohydrates are the primary source of energy for your body during exercise. When you eat carbohydrates, your body converts them into glucose, stored in your muscles and liver as glycogen. During exercise, your body breaks down glycogen to provide energy for your muscles. Carbohydrates also help maintain blood glucose levels during exercise, essential for avoiding fatigue and maintaining optimal performance.

Protein is essential for repairing and rebuilding muscle tissue, which can become damaged during intense exercise. Consuming protein after exercise can help speed up recovery and reduce muscle soreness. Protein also plays a role in supporting the immune system and maintaining healthy bones.

Fat is an essential source of energy during low to moderate-intensity exercise. It also helps your body absorb fat-soluble vitamins and provides essential fatty acids that it can't produce alone. Healthy fats like those in nuts, seeds, and fish can also help reduce inflammation and improve heart health.

To optimise your running performance and recovery, consuming the right balance of these macronutrients is important. Your specific needs will depend on your training goals, body type, and individual preferences.

Carb Loading for Marathons and Ultramarathons

Have you spent months training and preparing for an upcoming marathon or ultra run, only to hit a wall during the race? If so, you're not alone. Runners constantly suffer from "bonking," aka hitting a wall and gassing out mid-race.

But what if there was a science-backed way to improve performance that had nothing to do with running?

Enter carb loading! Carb loading is a popular practice among long-distance runners, and for a good reason. But what is carb loading, why is it important, and how can you do it correctly before race day?

What Is Carb Loading?

The goal with carb loading is simple: to improve performance by having more energy in your muscles as you start the race. It involves increasing carbohydrate intake in the days leading up to your race while tapering off other foods.

Why Is Carb Loading for Runners Important?

Carb loading helps runners by allowing the body to store more glycogen (a fuel source). Glycogen is the primary energy source used by our muscles during intense exercise, so it's crucial to ensure adequate amounts are available during your race.

This gives the body a reserve of energy to tap into during long runs, helping you avoid hitting the wall and powering through until the end. When done correctly, carb-loading before a marathon can give you an edge over the competition.

How to Carb Load for a Marathon or Ultra Run

Carb loading isn't about eating a massive bowl of pasta the night before your race. It's a gradual process, and it takes planning. Here are some tips for successful carb loading:

- Increase your carb intake gradually, starting 4-5 days before the race.
- Focus on complex carbohydrates. Three days before the race, aim to eat around 7-12 grams of carbohydrates per kilogram of lean body weight daily.
- Drink lots of water to stay hydrated. Drink around 8-10 glasses of water throughout the day before race day. This will help your body to flush out any toxins.

- Avoid excess fibre and protein, as these will slow carb-loading.
- Avoid high-fat foods as these will not provide enough long-term energy.

Foods To Eat When Carbohydrate Loading

When carb loading, it's important to focus on complex carbohydrates since they will provide a steady energy supply. Some foods to include in your carb-loading diet are:

- Whole wheat bread and other whole grains (some sources will suggest white bread and pasta, but I find it bloating and less nutrient dense!)
- Potatoes
- Oats
- Legumes such as beans, peas, and lentils
- Fruit such as apples and bananas
- Starchy vegetables like sweet potatoes, squash, and carrots

One final tip is perhaps seen as an unconventional one. Try introducing some sugary foods around three days before a race, as it's one of the best ways to get your glycogen stores up quickly! A personal favourite of mine is carb-loading with Oreos! A bag of Haribo is also a nice treat!

Stay Fuelled on Race Day

Carb loading isn't guaranteed to land you in the first place, but if done correctly, it can give you an edge over other runners that don't utilise it. With proper nutrition and hydration in the days leading up to a marathon or ultra race, you can ensure that your body is well-fueled and ready to go on race day.

The importance of hydration for running performance

Staying hydrated before, during, and after your runs is vital as a runner. Dehydration can lead to fatigue, decreased performance, and, in hot conditions, even worse! The human body comprises around 60% water, so it's crucial to replenish the fluids you lose through sweat and other bodily functions.

During exercise, the body produces sweat to help regulate its internal temperature. Sweating is the body's natural cooling mechanism, but it can also lead to significant fluid loss. As a result, it's crucial to drink fluids before, during, and after exercise to replenish the fluids lost through sweating.

In addition to water, replacing electrolytes lost through sweating is important. Electrolytes, such as sodium, potassium, and magnesium, are essential for maintaining proper hydration levels and ensuring optimal muscle function.

It's important to note that the recommended amount of water and electrolytes may vary based on your body type, weight, and training intensity. It's always best to consult with a sports nutritionist or dietitian to determine the appropriate amount of fluids and electrolytes needed for your needs.

Overall, proper hydration is essential for optimal running performance. Ensuring you consume the right amount of fluids and electrolytes before, during, and after your runs can help improve your performance, prevent dehydration, and support post-run recovery.

Chapter 2: Eating for Energy

The best foods to eat before and after runs

As a runner, fueling your body with the right foods is crucial to maximising your performance and enhancing your recovery. This means focusing on what you eat before and after your runs and consuming the proper daily nutrients.

Before your run, eating a meal rich in carbohydrates and moderate in protein and fat is crucial. Carbohydrates are essential for providing energy to your muscles, while protein and fat help to sustain that energy and keep you feeling full. Some pre-run meals include oatmeal with fruit and nuts, whole-grain toast with almond butter and banana, or a smoothie with yoghurt, fruit, and protein powder.

During your run, staying hydrated and replenishing your electrolytes are important. You can do this by drinking water or sports drinks and consuming energy gels or chews that provide a quick source of carbohydrates.

After your run, your body needs to recover and repair the muscles worked during your workout. This means consuming a meal high in protein and carbohydrates to help repair and rebuild those muscles. Some examples of post-run meals include a smoothie with Greek yoghurt, fruit, and protein powder, a quinoa and vegetable stir-fry with grilled chicken, or a turkey sandwich with whole-grain bread and avocado.

In addition to these pre- and post-run meals, consuming a well-rounded diet throughout the day is essential to provide your body with the nutrients it needs to function at its best. This includes consuming many fruits and vegetables, lean protein sources such as chicken, fish, and beans, and healthy fats like nuts, seeds, and avocado.

Paying attention to your body and adjusting your diet is also essential. Every runner is different, and what works for one person may not work for another. Pay attention to how your body feels after certain meals, and adjust accordingly.

By fueling your body with the right foods before and after your runs and maintaining a well-rounded diet throughout the day, you can optimise your performance, enhance your recovery, and feel your best both on and off the road.

Tips for fueling during long runs and races

As a runner, you know that proper fueling is critical to maintaining energy and optimal performance during long runs and races. But with so many options available, knowing what and how much to eat can be challenging. Here are some tips for fueling during long runs and races.

1. **Start fueling early:** The longer your run or race, the earlier you should start fueling. Aim to consume around 1 gram of carbohydrates per KG lean body weight per hour starting from the first hour of exercise. This can come from sports drinks, gels, chews, or other easily digestible carbohydrate sources.
2. **Practice, practice, practice:** It's important to practice fueling during your training runs so you can figure out what works best for you. Experiment with different types and amounts of fuel to see what your body responds to best. The gut CAN be trained!
3. **Don't forget to hydrate:** Proper hydration is essential for optimal performance, especially during long runs and races. Be sure to drink water regularly
4. **Don't try anything new on race day:** Stick to what you know works for you. This is not the time to try a new type of gel or sports drink you've never used before or have a breakfast you've never had before a long run. Stick to the fueling plan that you've practised during your training runs.
5. **Mix up your fuel sources:** In some races, such as ultramarathons, consuming various carbohydrate sources can help keep things exciting and prevent taste fatigue. Try alternating between sports drinks, gels, chews, and other easily digestible carbohydrate sources, and try real foods, too, for more extended events.
6. **Keep it simple:** The simpler the fuel, the easier it is for your body to digest and use, and it's also easier logistically! I see some people who are like a walking buffet and inevitably mess up their fuelling plan.
7. **Post-run fueling:** Remember to refuel after long runs and races to help your body recover and prepare for your next run. Aim to consume a carbohydrate-rich snack or meal within a couple of hours of finishing your run - the sooner, the better - and include protein to aid recovery.

Following these tips can help ensure you're fueling correctly during long runs and races and optimise your performance. Listen to your body and experiment with different fuel sources to find the best.

Nutrition For Long-Distance Runners

Ultrarunning is a gruelling sport testing the physical and mental limits of even the most experienced athletes. And as Ann Trason, a top ultrarunner and star of the bestselling book Born to Run, once said, "Ultrarunning is an eating and drinking competition." It's a statement that rings true for anyone who's ever struggled with a poor fuelling strategy and felt the crushing disappointment of a broken race.

That's why, as an experienced ultrarunner, I can't stress the importance of proper fuelling for endurance runners enough. And while it's undoubtedly crucial on race day, I firmly believe it's just as important in the days and weeks leading up to any long-distance event. After all, you can't expect to perform at your best if you only pay attention to your nutrition strategy on race day alone.

But let's focus now on the day of the race or those long training runs that serve as perfect opportunities to test different fuelling strategies. Indeed, what works for one runner may not work for another, so it's essential to experiment and find out what your body responds to best. And that's precisely what I aim to help you with in this section: providing tips and insights to help you develop a fuelling plan to support your endurance goals and help you achieve peak performance.

The Sciency bit

Firstly, some science... important science nonetheless, and whether you are into the sciency stuff or not, you need to know this, so stay with me... and we will focus solely on carbs here (stored in the muscles as glycogen). I am not a fan of keto (I tried it once, it was disgusting eating that much fat for a start, and, secondly, I got slower!) or fat-adapted running or fasted cardio stuff. This is about what is suitable for most people and, based on my experience, as a case study. If you are interested in fat adaptation or keto because that's what works for you, or you heard some bloke ran a 75467-mile race in 14 hours eating only olives and drinking melted butter, then you crack on and find that article because I am not going to reference them here, okay?!?!

We usually burn off 0.8-1g for females and 1-1.2g of carbohydrates per KG of body weight per hour. So if you are a 75kg runner with around 75-90g per hour of running, what does that look like in terms of food? 3 bananas or 3 scoops of most energy drink brands or 3 of most gels... you get the picture, and I am not saying you carry 12 bananas on a 4-hour run... unless you're a monkey?!!

We also need to consider the types of carbs... there are Fast Carbs (act very quickly and get into your system pretty much straight away, e.g., dried fruits, sugar, sweeties!) and Slow Carbs (slower to digest and release, e.g. pasta, bread, potatoes).

Finally, carbo-loading... in a nutshell, the stories of "pasta parties" and eating a boatload of carb-rich food the day/night before a big race are just plain dumb. You will bloat yourself for one, but eating an exorbitant amount of carbs the previous day does not fill up your glycogen stores. Instead, you should do this gradually over the course of the week before your big day; add in some rice, pasta, potatoes, etc. to each meal in that week (NOTE: do this WITHOUT increasing your overall calories – so hang back a touch on the protein intake) and race day your glycogen stores (which last about 90 minutes at marathon effort, longer if you run easier) will be nicely saturated.

What do I do for runs longer than 90 minutes, and WHEN should I take carbs in during my race/long run?

So, we have, as above, established that you need around 1g per KG of body weight to get you through each hour. Let's continue to work on a 75kg person in our examples, and it'll be a case of me using myself as that example since I weigh about that! This is a point I will touch on later... this is MY experience. YOUR experience may differ in terms of the foods you eat, covered below in the "WHAT should I eat" section.

Forget about intensity here; let's go with time spent running as the measure. Let's say my projected run time is 5 hours. Therefore, I am going to need 5x75g=375g carbs for the run. I like to break it down by hour and ensure that my carb intake is spread evenly, rather than having a big wallop of carbs in one hit and... in my pre-race preparations, I will use a spreadsheet to work it all out! Pretty geeky, but it's what works for me. You may want to write it down your fuelling plan and have it on you during the run, or maybe even have things in certain pockets of your shorts or race vest. Up to you to work that out!

Here is a screenshot of my spreadsheet for a recent race:

Hour #	hh:mm:ss	Item	Fast/Slow release Carb?	Total Gram of Carbs	Sweet/Savoury	Notes	Total carbs per hour
1	00:20:00	Bagel piece with PB&J	Slow	10	Savoury		75
	00:40:00	Gel	Fast	25	Sweet		
		500 ml with Energy & Electrolyte	Fast	40	Sweet	To be sipped gradually over the course of the hour	
2	01:20:00	Bagel piece with PB&J	Slow	10	Savoury		75
	01:40:00	Gel	Fast	25	Sweet		
		500 ml with Energy & Electrolyte	Fast	40	Sweet	To be sipped gradually over the course of the hour	
3	02:20:00	Bagel piece with PB&J	Slow	10	Savoury		75
	02:40:00	Gel	Fast	25	Sweet		
		500 ml with Energy & Electrolyte	Fast	40	Sweet	To be sipped gradually over the course of the hour	
4	03:20:00	piece of chocolate with sea salt	Fast	10	Sweet		75
	03:40:00	Gel	Fast	40	Sweet		
		500 ml with Energy & Electrolyte	Fast	25	Sweet	To be sipped gradually over the course of the hour	
5	04:20:00	piece of chocolate with sea salt	Fast	10	Savoury		75
	04:40:00	Gel	Fast	25	Sweet		
		500 ml with Energy & Electrolyte	Fast	40	Sweet	To be sipped gradually over the course of the hour	

As you can see, purely from a taste perspective, I like to mix it up in terms of sweet and savoury. Too many gels at the start of a race, and I feel disgusting by the latter stages, furry mouth feel! Something like a bagel works for me, and I also find it staves off hunger which is another consideration when running a long race. Nothing worse than being hungry in a race!

I also ensure that my SLOW release carbs (in my case, the bagel) is eaten early on. This is because the carbs from that will kick in towards the end of the race just when I need them most, whereas the gels kick in right away, and the energy drink is a constant intake of carbs.

For me, 500ml of fluid per hour works for my sweat rate, with 40g carbs worth of energy drink (usually around 2 scoops of something like Torq/Tailwind/Mountain Fuel etc.).

A bit of chocolate with Sea Salt is a game-changer for me! The little pinch of sea salt helps with salts lost through sweating and has the bonus of tasting DIVINE! Losing too much salt can lead to cramps and muscle spasms and end your race. I highly recommend the guys at Precision Hydration for all your sweaty needs!

You will also notice I start my fuelling around 20 mins into the race. It is essential to start eating from the start, DON'T WAIT. You start burning carbs almost immediately as your Heart Rate and effort levels go up, so you need to start replacing them immediately. Leave fuelling too late, at your peril!

What Should I Eat?

Well... now this is one of those unanswerable questions! There isn't really a prescribed "menu" for you to choose from here. As mentioned above, I have given you what works for ME, but I know some people who cannot stomach something like a bagel... I know people who cannot take gels as they give them the shits... I know people who will do a 100-mile ultra with just bars of chocolate... I know people who swear by Pork Pies or Vegan Sausage Rolls... I know people who eat pouches of baby food... You get the idea.

This is where I return to my earlier comment about testing foods, gels, powders etc., during your long training runs. They are an ideal opportunity to test stuff out and also to test out the eating & drinking strategy itself. Get used to eating what and when... get used to the mouthfeel of things... trust me, whilst I like a bagel, I now know that eating a bagel whilst pushing out 7:00min/mile pace is a goddamn choking hazard, so I always take a swig of drink with the bagel in my mouth to soften it up, and it slides down easier! You don't think of this stuff unless you experience and practise it!

So, to answer the question "What should I eat?"... that's up to you to find out. Just follow the grams per KG of bodyweight rule as above and enjoy learning how and what to eat whilst on the run! It can be a fun and sometimes exhilarating experience... especially when you have to dart behind a bush for a "nature poo"!

Finally... what about races under 90 minutes?

Answering this one in anticipation of the question! Well, as above, you store up to roughly 90 minutes worth of glycogen (assuming you have done carb-loading correctly, so in reality, you should not need any additional carbs, and, if you do, it should be fast carbs (gels, jelly babies, etc.). To give you my example of 5km to half marathon races:

– For 5km races (17-minute-ish PB), I take 1 gel 15 minutes before. Nothing in the race

– 10km races (36 minute-ish PB)... same as in 5km races

– Half marathon (79-minute-ish PB)... 1 gel 15 minutes before, then I often take a gel with 4 miles left. If I am really honest with myself, I think this is purely a psychological boost, which is not a bad thing

And, to cap things off... what about road marathons? As a sub-3 hour marathoner, I certainly wouldn't be eating solid foods. In my opinion, solid foods are reserved for trail races and ultra distances. Instead, I apply the 1g per KG bodyweight per hour rule, but I use gels starting from the 30-minute mark!

Chapter 3: Meal Planning and Grocery Shopping

How to plan your meals for the week

No matter how hard we try, it's almost impossible to eat the right things without a proper plan. The treat cupboard will get raided, and the shopping list will inevitably have a load of stuff you won't know what to do with!

Meal planning is a crucial aspect of my week... it takes me less than 10 minutes to plan out the week, saving me HOURS the rest of the week. Plus, I know I am eating the right things at the right times to fuel my running! By planning your meals ahead of time, you can save time and money, reduce food waste, and ensure that you always have healthy and nourishing food available.

Here are some tips for effective meal planning:

- **Choose your meals:** Open this book and start choosing some meals!
- **Keep it simple:** While it's great to experiment with new recipes and ingredients, it's also essential to keep things simple. I mean, do you need to have 7 different breakfasts?
- **Make a shopping list**: List all the ingredients you need for the week. This will help you avoid multiple grocery store trips and ensure you have everything you need to prepare your meals.
- **Consider your schedule**: Think about your schedule for the week and plan your meals accordingly. If you know you'll have a busy day, plan for a quick and easy meal that can be prepared in advance or on the go... there are plenty of those in this book!
- **Prep in advance:** To save time during the week, consider prepping some ingredients. Chop vegetables, cook grains, and portion out snacks, so they're ready to go when needed.
- **Be flexible:** Remember that meal planning is not set in stone. Be flexible and make adjustments as needed. If you eat out or have leftovers, adjust your weekly meal plan.

By following these tips, you can plan your meals effectively and ensure a healthy and balanced diet that fuels your runs and supports your overall health and well-being.

Chapter 4: Frequently Asked Questions and Troubleshooting

Common questions about nutrition and running performance

As a runner, having questions and concerns about your nutrition and how it affects your performance is common. This section will cover some frequently asked questions and provide troubleshooting tips for common issues.

Do I need to carb-load before a race?

Yes. But... it's not what many people think! You may have heard of pasta parties the day before a race! This is not an effective strategy. In fact, it's plain stupid. Carb-loading is a strategy runners use to maximise their glycogen stores before a race. While it can be helpful for longer races (half marathon or marathon distance), it's not always necessary for shorter distances.

Should I eat before morning runs?

Having some fuel before morning runs is essential to avoid running on an empty stomach, which can lead to low energy levels and decreased performance. If you don't have time for a full meal, try a light snack like a banana, an energy gel, or even some chocolate! As ever, find what's right for you!

Is it okay to eat right before a run?

Eating a full meal right before a run is generally not recommended, as it can cause digestive discomfort. However, some runners find that a small snack like a banana or energy gel can help give them a quick energy boost. You may also be training for a long ultramarathon where eating natural foods is necessary for your strategy. In this case, practice eating right before you run, as this can help train the gut for the demands of race day.

How do I know if I'm eating enough for my training?

Listening to your body and paying attention to hunger cues is essential. You could also track your food intake and ensure you get enough calories to fuel your runs and support recovery. Working with a registered dietitian can also help create a personalised nutrition plan for your training.

What should I eat after a run?

After a run, it's essential to replenish your glycogen stores and provide your body with the nutrients it needs to recover. A meal that includes carbohydrates, protein, and healthy fats is ideal. People often opt for a protein shake for convenience, but real food is better. There are lots of options in this book!

What are some healthy snack options for runners?

In this book... some healthy snack options for runners include fruits, vegetables, nuts and seeds, and protein bars. Choosing snacks that balance carbohydrates, protein, and healthy fats are important to keep you fueled and satisfied.

In summary, nutrition plays a crucial role in running performance, and paying attention to your diet is essential to ensure that you're properly fueling your runs and supporting recovery. If you have questions or concerns about your nutrition, don't hesitate to consult with a registered dietitian or nutritionist.

How to adjust your diet for injuries or illnesses

As a runner, it's crucial to maintain a healthy diet to fuel your training and keep your body strong. However, injuries and illnesses can sometimes get in the way and require adjustments to your nutrition plan. Here are some tips on adjusting your diet for injuries or illnesses.

Consult with a healthcare professional.

Before making any significant changes to your diet, it's essential to consult with a healthcare professional. They can provide personalised recommendations based on your specific condition and needs.

Adjust your calorie intake.

If you cannot exercise due to an injury or illness, you may need to adjust your calorie intake to reflect your lower energy needs. Make sure to eat a balanced diet, but consider reducing portions or cutting back on snacks.

On the other hand, if you're recovering from an injury or illness and your activity level is reduced, you may need to adjust your calorie intake to maintain your weight and energy levels. Consult a healthcare professional or registered dietitian to determine your appropriate calorie level.

Prioritise nutrient-dense foods

During times of injury or illness, it's important to prioritise nutrient-dense foods to support your recovery. Foods high in vitamins, minerals, and antioxidants can help strengthen your immune system and promote healing.

Focus on consuming various fruits, vegetables, lean proteins, whole grains, and healthy fats. This can help ensure you get multiple essential nutrients to support your recovery.

Adjust your macronutrient intake.

You may need to adjust your macronutrient intake depending on your injury or illness. For example, if you cannot exercise due to an injury, you may need to reduce your carbohydrate intake to reflect your lower energy needs.

On the other hand, if you're recovering from an illness, you may need to increase your protein intake to support muscle recovery and repair. Consult with a healthcare professional or a registered dietitian to determine the appropriate macronutrient ratio for your needs.

Stay hydrated

Proper hydration is vital for overall health and recovery. Ensure you drink plenty of water and other fluids throughout the day to help support your body's functions.

In some cases, such as with an illness that causes diarrhoea or vomiting, you may need to increase your fluid intake to prevent dehydration. Consult with a healthcare professional or a registered dietitian for specific recommendations.

Don't forget about mental health.

Injuries and illnesses can take a toll on mental health, and it's essential to prioritise your mental well-being and physical health - trust me, I know a lot about having to look after one's mental health!

In addition, seek support from loved ones or a mental health professional if you're struggling to cope with the challenges of an injury or illness (or anything for that matter!)

Adjusting your diet for injuries or illnesses requires careful consideration and consultation with a healthcare professional or a registered dietitian. Don't forget to prioritise your mental health as well as your physical health during these times.

Chapter 5 Breakfast

Biscoff Porridge

Let's start with one of my favourite breakfasts! I absolutely LOVE Biscoff, and this scratches the itch just nicely! It's also my go-to pre-long run/race breakfast because of the simple carbs in the spread and the slow release in the oats! Perfect!

Prepping Time: 5 mins - Cooking Time: 5 mins

INGREDIENTS

70g Fresh Raspberries

35g Lotus Biscoff ® / Speculoos Spread

15g Protein powder of choice (I love vanilla in this recipe!)

55g Rolled Porridge Oats

Pinch of cinnamon

INSTRUCTIONS

Mix the rolled porridge oats and double the amount of water (or milk if you prefer) in a bowl and microwave at medium-high heat for 2 minutes. Then stir in the Speculoos spread and pop back in the microwave for another minute

Allow the porridge to stand for a minute, then mix in the protein powder. Top with the raspberries and a pinch of cinnamon. Enjoy!

Oat and blueberry pancakes

Prepping Time: 10 mins - Cooking Time: 5 mins

Who doesn't love pancakes? These are healthy and delicious and are a great post-run brunch! The kids will love them too!

INGREDIENTS

10g Wheat flour

40g Oats

1 Banana

3 Eggs

Dash of Vanilla Essence

Pinch of Grated Lime Zest

10ml Honey or Maple Syrup

40g Fresh Blueberries

5m Olive oil

INSTRUCTIONS

Add the flour, oats, banana, eggs, and vanilla to a blender and blitz until the batter is smooth. Add half the honey/maple syrup and carefully fold some blueberries into the batter. Save a few for toppings.

Heat the oil in a frying pan over medium-high heat and add 2-3 tablespoons of the batter to fry one side until golden brown. Flip the pancake and fry until it turns golden on both sides. Repeat for the rest of the batter.

Serve the pancakes with honey/syrup, blueberries, and lime zest. Yum!

Bagel with smoked Salmon and cucumber

Prepping Time: 5 mins - Cooking Time: 0 mins

Super simple but super delicious, and Salmon has essential Omega-3 oils, which can ease inflammation, amongst other benefits! Great for those on the go!

INGREDIENTS

1 Plain or seeded bagel

50g Cream cheese

Pinch of fresh or dried dill

30g Thinly Sliced Cucumber

Small pinch of rocket leaves

50g Smoked salmon

INSTRUCTIONS

Toast your bagel. Whilst it's toasting, mix your cream cheese with the dill. Spread this on your toasted bagel, add the Salmon, cucumber, rocket and a crack of black pepper! Done!

Peanut butter overnight oats with strawberries and blueberries

Prepping Time: 5 mins - Cooking Time: 0 mins

Another absolute belter for a pre-long run or race day breakfast! Make it the night before so you can just grab it in the morning and eat!

INGREDIENTS

20g Peanut butter (Get a good quality PB, not the nasty cheap stuff!)

80g Skimmed milk or Oat Milk

70g Fat-free Greek Yoghurt

60g Rolled Porridge Oats

10g Honey

40g Fresh Strawberries, sliced

20g Fresh Blueberries

10g crushed walnuts

INSTRUCTIONS

Mix the oats with the yoghurt and milk in a breakfast bowl and stir well. Cover and place in the fridge overnight (this bit is important!!). Next morning, if it needs more liquid then add a dash more milk and stir.

Warm the PB in the microwave for just a few seconds (its easier to drizzle over!), top the oats with the PB, Strawberries, Blueberries, Honey and Walnuts. Eat!

Scrambled egg and Avo on toast!

Prepping Time: 5 mins - Cooking Time: 10 mins - Servings: 1

Simple, but delicious breakfast that I love as a weekend post-run meal. After years in my hospitality career of seeing terrible scrambled eggs, it's a bug bear of mine when they aren't delicious and creamy! Follow this recipe for perfect scrambled egg!

INGREDIENTS

½ Avocado

2 Slices of Bread (I prefer sourdough)

3 Eggs

10g butter

Sprinkle of chopped fresh parsley and chives

INSTRUCTIONS

Put your bread in the toaster and get that toasting! Crack the eggs, whisk with a fork and season to taste with salt and pepper, then pour into a nonstick pan with the butter. Stir constantly at a medium heat until they have thickened but still have a certain creaminess about them! Trust me, they will be divine!

Take your toast out, put onto your plate and mash your avocado onto the toast. Top with the scrambled eggs and sprinkle on the chives and parsley. Another crack of black pepper will set this off just nicely!

Biscoff Breakfast cheesecake

Prepping Time: 5 mins - Cooking Time: 0 mins

Told you I love Biscoff! Another easy breakfast that you can make in batches to save you time during the week.

INGREDIENTS

50g Raspberries

100g Zero fat Greek yoghurt

50g Low Fat Cream Cheese

5 Lotus Biscoff Biscuits

10g Maple Syrup

Pinch of Cinnamon

INSTRUCTIONS

Smash up the biscuits in a freezer bag until roughly fine and put them in a nice glass or jam jar!

Mix your cream cheese, yoghurt, maple and cinnamon together and scoop it on top of the biscuits. Top off with your raspberries and enjoy!

Protein pancakes with nut butter and banana

Prepping Time: 10 mins - Cooking Time: 30 mins - Servings: 1

INGREDIENTS

25g Protein powder

100ml Almond milk

70g Porridge Oats

90ml (about 3 eggs worth) Egg whites

10ml olive oil

20g nut butter

1 banana

5g chia seeds

INSTRUCTIONS

In a food processor/blender, whizz up the protein powder (ideally vanilla) with the egg whites, almond milk and porridge oats until you get a smooth batter

Heat the oil in a frying pan on a medium-high heat. Pour enough batter in to make a pancake about the size of the palm of your hand. Fry until bubbling on top, flip over and repeat the other side. Do this for all the batter

Drizzle your peanut butter, slice the banana and sprinkle the chia seeds on top of the pancakes and devour!!

Dark chocolate overnight oats

Prepping Time: 5 mins - Cooking Time: Overnight

Chocolate for breakfast….? Absolutely! The benefits of a good quality dark chocolate are no secret, plus the hit of carbs from the chocolate and the oats make this another great pre-long run breakfast!

INGREDIENTS

15g good quality dark chocolate (over 70% cocoa)

100ml Skimmed milk or plant milk

100g zero fat Greek yoghurt

10g Cocoa powder

50g Rolled Porridge Oats

40g raspberries

INSTRUCTIONS

Mix in your bowl the milk, oats, yoghurt and cocoa powder. Cover and place in the fridge overnight.

Take out of the fridge the next morning, top with the raspberries and grate the dark chocolate over it all and enjoy!

Veggie Breakfast "Fry Up"

Prepping Time: 5 mins - Cooking Time: 20 mins

You know, sometimes I just want a big breakfast after a long run. But to keep it on the "healthy" side, I love this veggie version of the British classic fry up!

INGREDIENTS

¼ can Baked Beans in tomato sauce

10 Cherry tomatoes, halved

5 Mushrooms, Quartered

2 slices bread of your choice

3 Plant-based Sausages of your choice

10g butter or plant-based spread

Sprinkle of chopped parsley

INSTRUCTIONS

Preheat the oven to 200°C (180°C Fan). Place the sausages, mushrooms and cherry tomatoes on a lined baking tray (or a fancy oven safe pan!) and cook according to the instructions on the pack of sausages.

Add the baked beans to a saucepan to warm through for 5 minutes at a medium heat, stirring regularly.

Toast the bread and butter it, then serve the sausages, cherry tomatoes, mushrooms and baked beans on top. Season with salt and pepper and sprinkle the parsley all over.

Cinnamon and raisin bagel with PB, Jam and banana

Prepping Time: 5 mins - Cooking Time: 0 mins

Another pre-run staple for me! Eaten 30 mins beforehand, a simple toasted bagel with banana and jam is a quick fix to set me up for a morning run

INGREDIENTS

1 Cinnamon and Raisin Bagel, toasted

20g Strawberry Jam

20g Peanut Butter

Half a sliced banana

INSTRUCTIONS

Toast the bagel and then spread the peanut butter on one side, jam on the other, put the sliced banana in the middle and eat!

Chapter 6 Lunch

Smokey BBQ Chicken Nachos

Prepping Time: 10 mins - Cooking Time: 15 mins

Some of the top ultrarunners in the world (Camille Herron, Courtney Dauwalter) are famed for their love of nachos to fuel their running exploits! This makes a great lunch and takes me back to my days working in an American Bar & Grill!

INGREDIENTS

1 Red onion, diced

60g plain tortilla chips

100g Chicken breast fillet, diced up in small chunks

30g barbecue sauce

20g mature cheddar cheese

1 Tomato, diced

1 clove garlic, crushed and finely chopped

5ml olive oil

1 teaspoon Smoked Paprika

½ teaspoon cayenne pepper (optional depending on how hot you like it!)

INSTRUCTIONS

Preheat your oven to 180°C (160 fan).

In a frying pan, heat the olive oil over a medium heat and add the chicken and fry for 2 mins. Add the garlic, paprika, salt and pepper. Fry until the chicken is no longer pink in the middle then add the barbecue sauce, heating gently until its warmed through.

Next, on a baking tray, evenly place half the tortilla chips, top with half the chicken, then half the cheese and lastly half the diced onion. Repeat with the second layer until all the ingredients are used up.

Bake in the oven for 5-10 minutes. The cheese should be melted!

Get stuck in with your hands and enjoy this epic lunch!

Tuna pasta salad with tomato, peppers and olives

Prepping Time: 10 mins - Cooking Time: 15 mins

A powerhouse of a lunch that you can prep ahead, take to work for lunch or eat a la carte! Pasta is a go-to carb source for us runners and it's a dish full of nutrients to fuel our training! Nigella Seeds are said to be excellent for reducing inflammation!

INGREDIENTS

80g Whole wheat pasta, uncooked

10ml Olive oil

1 Green pepper

1 Red pepper

5 cherry tomatoes, halved

5 large green olives, halved, pitted

½ Can Tuna in spring water

Juice of ¼ lemon

15g rocket leaves and sprinkle of Nigella Seeds

INSTRUCTIONS

Cook the pasta according to the instructions on the packet in a pot of lightly salted boiling water. When ready, turn the heat off and drain the water. Put the cooked pasta back in the pan and add the olive oil immediately and stir, this will not only dress the pasta but it'll stop it from going sticky!

Drain the tuna, slice and dice the peppers. Add them into the pasta along with the tomatoes, olives and rocket leaves. Stir it all together and season with the lemon juice and salt and pepper to taste. For an additonal flavour and nutrient boost, chop some fresh basil and parsley finely and stir that in too! Sprinkle on the Nigella Seeds!

Crispy herby chicken and mango wrap

Prepping Time: 10 mins - Cooking Time: 15 mins

A solid lunch that veers away from a boring old sandwich! Great protein hit, nutritious whole-grain carbs from the tortillas and super herbs and mango bringing the flavour!

INGREDIENTS

1 small red onion, finely diced

2 Wholemeal tortilla (or white if you prefer)

100g - Chicken breast fillet, finely sliced

10ml olive oil

1 teaspoon mixed dried herbs

Handful chopped lettuce

Handful chopped parsley

30g mature Cheddar cheese, grated

2 teaspoons mango chutney

INSTRUCTIONS

Season the chicken with salt and pepper. Heat a pan over medium heat with the olive oil. Add the chicken and fry for 2 mins, then add the mixed dried herbs and cook until the chicken is no longer pink in the middle.

Lay the tortillas flat and spread 1 teaspoon of the mango chutney on one wrap, the other on the other! Divide the herby chicken between the two, add the cheese, lettuce and parsley, then roll each into a tightly wrapped wrap!

Add each wrap to a nonstick pan at a medium-high heat and cook, seam side down first, until its is golden brown, carefully flip it over and cook the other side. Serve and enjoy your crispy delicious wraps!!

Omelette with veggies

Prepping Time: 5 mins - Cooking Time: 15 mins

The good old-fashioned omelette! I still make mine the way my great grandmother taught me which makes them go really fluffy! Protein, fats and carbs in this make it one of my go-to simple lunches

INGREDIENTS

100g Mushrooms (button, white or chestnut)

1-2 slices Whole grain bread

80g Green beans, trimmed and cut into 1cm long pieces

Handful of Washed, Fresh Spinach

3 Eggs, whole and whisked

10ml olive oil

Pinch dried tarragon and parsley

INSTRUCTIONS

In a small pot, add in the green beans, add just enough water to cover them and boil gently until tender. Set aside to dry off.

Slice your mushrooms and add them to a preheated pan on a high heat with the oil. Its almost impossible to burn mushrooms, so don't worry about the high heat of the pan. Don't be tempted to move the mushrooms around too much, this makes them go watery! Top tip there!

Once the mushrooms are nicely browned, turn them a little and add the tarragon and parsley, then add in the green beans, fry them for a minute then add in the whisked eggs. Season with salt and black pepper

Once the bottom of the omelette is starting to go a golden brown, take it off the heat and put the pan under a hot grill to cook the top until that's starting to go golden brown in places too

Serve the cooked omelette on top of the bed of spinach, season with salt and pepper again if desired and eat with your bread!

Lunchtime Raw Mega Salad

Prepping Time: 10 mins - Cooking Time: 15 mins

Sometimes I will make a large batch of this salad and have it for multiple lunch days in a row for convenience. Its all using raw ingredients so has amazing crunch as well as nutritional value! The dressing makes it moreish!

INGREDIENTS

2 spring onions

2 radishes

1 peeled carrot

½ can chickpeas

½ can blackeyed beans

125g tinned sweetcorn

10 cherry tomatoes

30g cucumber

½ red bell pepper, deseeded

½ yellow bell pepper, deseeded

Handful fresh parsley, coriander, basil

Dressing:

15ml olive oil

10ml apple cider vinegar

1 teaspoon Dijon mustard

1 teaspoon honey

1 teaspoon Smoked Paprika

INSTRUCTIONS

Simply, roughly chop all the vegetables, finely chop the herbs, drain and rinse the sweetcorn, beans and chickpeas and add to a large bowl and mix together

Whisk the olive oil, apple cider vinegar, Dijon mustard, honey, paprika, salt and pepper together and pour into the salad mix, coat everything and enjoy!

Chicken & Avocado pasta salad

Prepping Time: 5 mins - Cooking Time: 20 mins

INGREDIENTS

½ a Red pepper, de-seeded and diced

½ avocado, ripe

75g - Pasta, uncooked

120g Chicken breast fillet, sliced

Handful of Spinach, roughly chopped

Handful of lettuce, roughly chopped

1 teaspoon smoked paprika

½ teaspoon dried oregano

½ teaspoon dried thyme

5ml olive oil

Juice of ½ Lemon

INSTRUCTIONS

Cook the pasta according to the instructions on the packet in a pot of lightly salted water.

Fry the chicken with the olive oil, paprika, thyme and oregano over a medium-high heat until it is golden and cooked through. Once the chicken is cooked, add the red pepper, fry for a few minutes more. Remove from the heat and add in the cooked pasta, squeeze the lemon juice all over and give it all a mix together. Season with salt and pepper to taste.

Cut the avocado in half and remove the stone. Use a spoon to scoop out the flesh and dice it up into rough chunks and add to the mixture, gently stir it through.

Serve and enjoy!

Salmon, little trees, feta, and pasta

Prepping Time: 5 mins - Cooking Time: 15 mins

Yeah, sounds a weird combo, but trust me, this is delicious! You've also got a great meal for days where you've done a hard session or long run... Salmon for healthy fats and protein, broccoli is a total superstar of a veggie, the pasta for the carbs, and the sharpness of the feta goes great with the fish! Enjoy!

INGREDIENTS

70g Pasta, uncooked

100g Broccoli florets

80g Salmon fillet

25g feta cheese

10ml Olive oil

½ teaspoon dried or fresh chopped dill

Juice of ½ a lemon

INSTRUCTIONS

Cook the pasta according to the instructions on the packet in a pot of lightly salted water. 3-4 mins before the pasta is finished cooking, add your broccoli florets into the water to cook with the pasta. Drain the water off and toss in the olive oil to stop the pasta from sticking.

Meanwhile, fry the salmon skin side down in a non-stick pan on a medium to high heat. Cook until the skin starts to go crispy, then cook flesh side down until starting to brown and repeat this until it is cooked through. Be careful not to overcook though!

Break the Salmon up roughly with a fork, add to the pasta and broccoli, squeeze in your lemon juice and sprinkle in the dill and give it a gentle stir to mix. Serve onto your plate, then crumble the feta over it

Season with salt and cracked black pepper to taste!

Chicken fajita wrap with quick guacamole

Prepping Time: 10 mins - Cooking Time: 10 mins

Another recipe that takes me back to my early years working in an American grill. The waiters would walk through the entire restaurant with the fajitas sizzling away on a hot skillet creating amazing smells throughout the place! It was quite a showpiece too!

INGREDIENTS

2 Wholemeal tortilla wraps

100g Chicken breast fillet, thinly sliced

1 Green bell pepper, deseeded and sliced

1 Red bell pepper, deseeded and sliced

1 small red onion

½ avocado

2-3 cherry tomatoes

Juice of a ¼ lime

5ml olive oil

½ teaspoon each of smoked paprika, garlic powder, ground cumin, ground coriander and dried oregano

INSTRUCTIONS

Season the chicken with the spices mix, salt and pepper and toss through in a bowl.

Fry the chicken in a pan with the oil, peppers and onions over high heat for approximately 5-7 minutes or until the chicken is cooked

For your guacamole, smash up the avocado flesh in a bowl with a fork, squeeze in your lime juice and season with salt and pepper. Chop the tomatoes finely and add that in too. Give it a good mix!

Warm the tortillas according to the instructions on the packet.

Spread the guacamole mix on top of the warm tortillas, then scoop in your fajita mix and roll into a wrap. You can also add a sprinkle of grated cheddar cheese too if you want an extra layer of flavour!

Enjoy!

Japanese Poke bowl with Salmon

Prepping Time: 10 mins - Cooking Time: 20 mins

Given that my wife works for a well-known Sushi restaurant chain, I couldn't not include a Poke Bowl! I've devoured many of these, especially during my carb loading days!

INGREDIENTS

80g white rice, uncooked

60g Smoked Salmon (or ideally if you can get sushi grade raw Salmon then that's ideal! DO NOT BE TEMPTED TO TRY USING NORMAL RAW SALMON!!)

30g Edamame beans, frozen

½ ripe avocado, sliced

30g Cucumber, diced

30g Radish, sliced

5ml Sesame oil

10ml Rice Vinegar

10ml Mirin

Pinch of Sesame Seeds

20g Diced Spring onion

INSTRUCTIONS

Cook your rice according to the instructions on the packet. When it is done cooking, drain and then add in sesame oil, Mirin and Rice Vinegar and give it a good mix! Place in a bowl

Whilst the rice is cooking, cook the edamame beans in a pan of hot water for 4-5 minutes. Drain them off and place in the bowl with the rice

Top with the avocado, cucumber, radish and Salmon. If using the smoked Salmon tear it into strips. If you can get sushi grade salmon, then cut into 1cm cubes and add into the bowl

Sprinkle with the sesame seeds and spring onions and enjoy!

Chapter 7 Snacks

Beetroot Hummus

Again, the magical beetroot comes in to play here! Mixed into a simple, but delicious hummus recipe, this is a great mid-afternoon or post run snack!

INGREDIENTS

2 medium, ready cooked beetroots

1 can of chickpeas, drained and rinsed

2 cloves of garlic, minced

2 tablespoon tahini paste

2 tablespoon freshly squeezed lemon juice

40-50ml olive oil

1 teaspoon ground cumin

Salt and pepper to taste

Paprika, for garnish (optional)

INSTRUCTIONS

Add the beetroots, chickpeas, garlic, tahini, lemon juice, olive oil, and cumin to a food processor.

Blend until the mixture is smooth and creamy, scraping down the sides of the bowl as necessary. Season with salt and pepper to taste.

Transfer the hummus to a serving bowl and sprinkle paprika on top (optional). Serve with your favorite vegetables, pita bread, or crackers. Enjoy!

Energy Balls!

I make these in batches and use them before a run or on long trail runs and races. They pack a massive punch of energy as well as good nutrients! They freeze well too, just take them out the night before your run and pop them in a freezer bag for your run!

INGREDIENTS

100g Oats

50g Peanut Butter

2 ripe Bananas

30g Honey

30g Pitted dates

30g Mixed Chopped Nuts (Almonds, Walnuts, etc.)

1 tsp Cinnamon

2 tbsp Cocoa Powder

Pinch of Pink Himalayan Salt

3 tbsp Water

INSTRUCTIONS

Chuck everything other than the water in a food processor. Whilst blending, gradually add the water until you get a very sticky dough.

Once you have your dough, use your hands to form the mixture into balls, about 2 cm in diameter.

Place the balls on a tray lined with parchment paper and chill in the fridge for 30 minutes.

Serve chilled or store in an airtight container in the fridge for up to a week or freezer for up to a month. Enjoy as a pre, mid or post-run snack!

Salted Chocolate Fudge Flapjack!

Another one I make in batches and use them before a run or on long trail runs and races! Chewy delicious goodness to fuel your running! Or simply enjoy it as a snack with a cup of tea or coffee!

INGREDIENTS

200g Rolled Oats
125g Unsalted Butter
60g Brown Sugar
30g dark chocolate chips
30g mini caramel fudge chunks (usually in the baking section of supermarkets!)
4 tbsp Golden Syrup
1 tsp Vanilla Extract
Pinch of Pink Himalayan Salt

INSTRUCTIONS

Preheat your oven to 180°C (160°C fan). Grease a 20cm square baking tin and line with baking parchment.

In a saucepan, melt the butter, brown sugar, golden syrup, vanilla extract, and salt together over low heat until the sugar has dissolved.

Remove the saucepan from heat and stir in the oats until evenly coated. Then stir in the chocolate chips and fudge pieces

Spoon the mixture into the prepared tin and use a fork to spread and flatten it evenly.

Bake in the preheated oven for 25-30 minutes, or until the flapjack is golden brown and firm to the touch.

Allow the flapjack to cool for 10 minutes in the tin, then cut into bars or squares while still warm.

Leave the flapjack to cool completely in the tin, then transfer to an airtight container. Serve and enjoy!

Banging Banana Bread!

Inspiration taken from a recipe my wife uses. Bananas are a runners best friend and this scratches the itch to have something sweet! Take a slice on a long trail run with you! Yum!

Ingredients:

200g Plain Flour

1 tsp Baking Powder

1/2 tsp Baking Soda

1/4 tsp Pink Himalayan Salt

2 ripe Bananas, mashed

100g Brown Sugar

2 Large Eggs

100g Melted Butter

1 tsp Vanilla Extract

100g Chopped Walnuts (optional)

Instructions:

Preheat the oven to 180°C (160°C fan. Grease a 20cm x 10cm loaf tin.

In a large bowl, whisk together the flour, baking powder, baking soda, and salt.

In a separate bowl, mix together the mashed bananas, brown sugar, eggs, melted butter, and vanilla extract until well combined.

Pour the wet mixture into the dry mixture and mix until just combined.

Fold in the chopped walnuts (if using).

Pour the batter into the prepared tin and smooth the top and bake in the preheated oven for 50-60 minutes, or until a toothpick inserted into the center comes out clean.

Allow the banana bread to cool in the tin for 10 minutes, then transfer to a wire rack to cool completely.

Serve and enjoy as a pre-early morning run or as a snack!

Runners Trail Mix

Trail mix was originally developed as a tasty and nutritious snack for hikers! My simple trail mix has runners in mind and is ideal for those long runs out on the trails!

INGREDIENTS

200g mixed nuts (almonds, walnuts, cashews, macadamia is my favourite mix)
100g dried fruit (you can use raisins, cranberries, apricots, etc.)
50g seeds (sunflower, pumpkin, etc.)
100g banana chips
50g chocolate chips
1 tsp Pink Himalayan sea salt

INSTRUCTIONS

Mix all ingredients together, give it a shake or stir, and store in an airtight container for up to a month.

Enjoy your homemade trail mix as a snack on-the-go or even as a topping for yogurt or porridge!

Protein powered cheese toastie!

Prepping Time: 10 mins - Cooking Time: 0 mins

Who doesn't love a cheese toastie?! A bit of an indulgent one, but the addition of the cottage cheese (which is high in Casein protein) gives that extra protein punch. Great to have on a speedwork run day!

INGREDIENTS

2 slices wholemeal bread

30g Cottage cheese with chives (fat free ideally)

30g Mature Cheddar Cheese. grated

10g finely diced red onion or spring onion

Splash of Worcestershire sauce

INSTRUCTIONS

Toast the bread on both sides.

Then place both cheeses, onions and the Worcestershire sauce on one slice of and melt it under a hot grill.

Once melted, put the other slice of bread on, slice the sandwich in half and eat!

Eat the sandwich and cottage cheese

Skyr with fruit

Prepping Time: 5 mins - Cooking Time: 0 mins

Superb protein hit, quick to make and full of vitamins and nutrients. Ideal for a post-run or afternoon snack

INGREDIENTS

225g Skyr Icelandic Yoghurt

1 Banana, sliced

60g Blueberries

Segments from 1 orange (used tinned Mandarins if that's easier)

1 kiwi, diced

Drizzle of honey

5g Chia seeds

INSTRUCTIONS

Add the skyr to a bowl. Top with the berries, banana, orange amd kiwi. Drizzle the honey over the top and sprinkle the chia seeds

Chapter 8 Smoothies and Bowls

Blueberry and peanut butter smoothie

Prepping Time: 5 mins - Cooking Time: 0 mins

This is so yummy! Blueberries provide crucial antioxidants which help remove toxins and waste products from the body. Great recovery boost!

INGREDIENTS

15g Peanut butter

150g zero fat Greek yoghurt

125g Frozen Blueberries

10ml Honey or Maple Syrup

INSTRUCTIONS

Put all ingredients in a blender. Blitz until smooth. Add extra water or milk if too thick

Serve and drink!

Berry Fro-Yo!

Prepping Time: 10 mins - Cooking Time: 0 mins

Frozen yoghurt!! Yessss! I love this as a snack or treat. It scratches the itch when wanting something sweet but is also super high in protein which is great for recovery from those hard running sessions!

INGREDIENTS

80g Frozen Raspberries

100g Frozen Strawberries

150g Skyr yoghurt (strawberry flavour ideally but plain also fine!)

20ml Maple syrup or honey

INSTRUCTIONS

Put all ingredients in a food processor or blender. Blend until you get a nice thick ice cream texture. Scoop into a bowl and devour!

Berry "Power" bowl

Prepping Time: 5 mins - Cooking Time: 0 mins

Based on the popular Acai Bowl trend, this super berry power bowl will give you a superb protein and energy hit! Full of amazing nutrients too!

INGREDIENTS

20g Coconut chips

50g Pineapple Pieces

150g Skyr (a low-fat strained Icelandic yoghurt!)

1 Banana, Peeled and Sliced

150g mixed frozen berries

15g crushed nuts of your choice (I love macadamia!)

15g Chia seeds

INSTRUCTIONS

Blend up the frozen berries with the Skyr until super smooth and pour into a bowl. Top with the sliced banana, pineapple, coconut chips, crushed nuts and the chia seeds... why not add a sprig of mint too, very chef-y!

Super smooth fruit and nut bowl

Prepping Time: 10 mins - Cooking Time: 0 mins

INGREDIENTS

100ml Almond Milk

100g fat free Greek yoghurt

125g Mixed Frozen Berries

1 Banana, peeled

30g porridge oats

20g Peanut butter

15g Protein powder (vanilla or strawberry is ideal)

Toppings of your choosing – I like chia seeds, coconut chips and sliced strawberries!

INSTRUCTIONS

Add everything to the blender, whizz up until smooth. Pour into a bowl. Top with your favourite toppings, Enjoy!

Choconana smoothie!!

Prepping Time: 10 mins - Cooking Time: 0 mins

Simple, delicious, energy booster! Get in!!!

INGREDIENTS

2 bananas

10 Whole almonds

15ml Maple syrup

20g Cocoa powder

200-300ml plant milk

INSTRUCTIONS

Add all ingredients to a blender. Blend until smooth. Drink!

Super smoothie

Prepping Time: 5 mins - Cooking Time: 0 mins

Smoothie... so convenient, quick to make and you can pack goodness into them as well as flavour! Keeping frozen fruit in the freezer make these an easy go-to option when you need a quick fix! Beetroot is an incredible food for runners because of its nitrate content!

INGREDIENTS

1 Banana, peeled

100g Strawberries, frozen

100g Raspberries, frozen

50g blueberries, frozen

1 cooked beetroot

Handful of spinach

5g chia seeds

5g flax seeds, cold milled

Optional – add in green powders like spirulina or chlorella for an extra massive boost of nutrients (the colour will look a bit gross, but a small price to pay for the nutritional value!)

INSTRUCTIONS

Peel the banana. Add all ingredients and some water to a blender (I prefer using the Nutribullet). Blend until super smooth. Add some more water or ice cubes to get the desired texture, if needed, and blend again.

Drink!!

Berry smoothie with chocolate

Prepping Time: 5 mins - Cooking Time: 0 mins

All hail the chocolate!! This is a delicious combination that'll help recover from those quality running session!

INGREDIENTS

150g Skyr
80g Blueberries, frozen
80g Raspberries, frozen
50g Oats
30g good quality dark chocolate, min 70% cocoa

INSTRUCTIONS

Add all ingredients and some water to a blender (I prefer using the Nutribullet). Blend until super smooth. Add some plant milk, water or ice cubes to get the desired texture, if needed, and blend again. Drink!

Chapter 9 Dinner

Butter chicken with rice and naan

Prepping Time: 10 mins - Cooking Time: 30 mins

I love a curry and this is up there with the G.O.A.T's of all the curries! All the lovely spices have amazing nutritional properties, it's full of much needed calories without it being like a greasy takeaway curry! I particularly like this on a Saturday night after having done a Saturday long-run!

INGREDIENTS

100g Chicken thigh, boneless and skinless

20g Butter

1 small white onion

¼ can chopped tomatoes

15g tomato puree

2 cloves garlic, minced

1 tbsp grated ginger

1 tbsp garam masala

1 tsp ground turmeric

1 tsp ground cumin

1 tsp paprika

1 tsp chili powder (optional)

50g Greek yoghurt, fat free

Handful coriander leaves, chopped

40g brown basmati rice

1 small naan bread

INSTRUCTIONS

Cook the rice to the instructions on the packet.

In a large pan, melt the butter over a medium heat. Add the chopped onion, minced garlic, and grated ginger. Cook until the onion is soft and translucent.

Add the garam masala, turmeric, cumin, paprika, and chili powder to the pan. Stir to combine.

Add the chicken to the pan and cook until browned on all sides.

Pour in your chopped tomatoes and bring the mixture to a boil. Reduce heat to low and let it simmer for 10-20 minutes or until the sauce has thickened slightly. Watch it doesn't go too dry!

Turn the heat off and stir in the Greek yoghurt. It's important to do this with the heat off otherwise the yoghurt will curdle!

Season the curry with salt and cracked black pepper to taste.

Serve the butter chicken curry over the rice and garnish with fresh coriander leaves. Heat the naan bread according to the instructions on the packet.

Serve the chicken with the naan, rice and enjoy!

Lasagne

Prepping Time: 10 mins - Cooking Time: 50 mins

After working for Jamie Oliver, you'd think I would have come away with some more fancy love of different pastas! But I used to go back time and again for the Lasagne on the menu! My recipe is without the white sauce to dial back the calorific, fatty content... it also makes it easier to put together!

INGREDIENTS

250g Lean beef mince

200g Wholemeal Lasagne sheets

1 carrot, 1 stick of celery, 1 small red onion – all very finely diced

10ml olive oil

40g Mature Cheddar Cheese

20g parmesan cheese

1 tin Chopped tomatoes.

1 heaped tablespoon of Dried Italian Mixed Herbs

INSTRUCTIONS

Preheat the oven to 200°C (180°C fan).

First, in a large pan with the olive oil on a medium heat, fry the diced carrot, celery and onion mix (in Italy they call this Sofrito!) until beginning to soften

Add the mince and season with salt, pepper and the herbs until the meat is cooked through. Darin any excess liquid.

Then add the chopped tomatoes, heat through and then set aside.

To build the lasagne, spoon a layer of the meat sauce into a square ovenproof dish, then add the lasagne sheets and a sprinkle of cheese. Repeat this until you have used up all the ingredients. Make sure the lasagne sheets are well covered in the sauce so they absorb the sauce!

Top with any remaining grated cheese, the parmesan and then cook the lasagne in the oven for 35-45 minutes until the cheese on top is bubbling and golden.

Allow to cool, for at least 20 minutes before serving. It keeps well in the fridge for up to 3 days or in the freezer for a month

Peri Peri chicken and zingy rice

Prepping Time: 30 mins - Cooking Time: 30 mins

Who doesn't love a "cheeky" Peri Peri chicken from a certain high street chicken chain here in the UK?! This will tickle your taste buds and provide you with lots of nutrition from the herbs and spices, protein from the chicken and carbs from the veggies and rice!

INGREDIENTS

120g - Chicken breast, whole

15ml Olive oil

1 red bell pepper deseeded and roughly chopped.

1 medium Courgette deseeded and roughly chopped.

½ teaspoon Cayenne pepper

½ teaspoon Ginger, ground

½ teaspoon Onion powder

½ teaspoon Garlic powder

1 ½ teaspoon Paprika

½ teaspoon Oregano, dried

70g basmati rice, uncooked (for this recipe I prefer white rice, but brown is also good and more nutritional being a whole grain!)

Juice of ½ a Lime

1 Pod of Cardamom

1 Pc - Star anise

INSTRUCTIONS

Cook the rice as per the packet instructions, but add into the pot of lightly salted water the star anise and the cardamom pod whilst the rice cooks to take on their flavour!

Place your chicken (no need to slice it) in a bowl along with the Peri Peri seasoning (paprika, oregano, cayenne, garlic powder, onion powder, ground ginger, salt and pepper and 5ml of the oil) give it a good coating, cover the bowl, and let it marinate in the fridge for at least 30 minutes or, ideally, overnight.

Preheat the oven to 200°C (gas) or 180°C (fan). Place the pepper and courgette on a baking tray, pour over the olive oil and give it a toss to cover. Season with salt and pepper and place in the oven.

Meanwhile, fry the chicken on each side for 2-3 minutes over a medium-high heat until it start to go golden on each side.

Remove the chicken from the pan and place it on top of the peppers and courgettes and cook for roughly another 12- 15 minutes until the chicken is cooked through.

For the rice. Finish it by draining any excess water, remove the cardamom and star anise. Sprinkle over the lime juice, give it a good stir and serve on the side with your chicken and veggies!

King prawn soft tacos

Prepping Time: 15 mins - Cooking Time: 10 mins

Super quick, super delicious and one the whole family can easily enjoy... and get messy with!

INGREDIENTS

3 Small Corn tortillas

1 small red onion, diced finely

1 red or green bell pepper (or half of each!), diced into small chunks

½ tin drained sweetcorn

120g peeled, deveined King Prawns

1 teaspoon each dried oregano, ground coriander, ground cumin

2-3 Garlic clove, minced

30g Cheddar Cheese, grated

Hot pepper sauce to taste

Squeeze of Lime Juice to taste

10 chopped cherry tomatoes

Handful chopped fresh coriander leaves

15ml olive oil

INSTRUCTIONS

Heat a pan with the oil on a high heat and fry the onion, garlic and oregano with the spices for 2 minutes. Add the bell pepper and sweetcorn and fry for another 2 minutes

Add in the prawns and cook until they turn a beautiful pink colour and don't overcook them! Season to taste with salt, pepper and oregano. Take of the heat and serve in a serving bowl!

Warm your tortillas as per the packet

Lay a tortilla flat and scoop in the prawn mix, some cheese, some hot pepper sauce (if you like the heat) a squeeze of lime juice, some tomatoes and a sprinkle of coriander leaves. Roll up and devour!!

Beef Panang Curry

Prepping Time: 10 mins - Cooking Time: 20 mins

I am not massive on red meat (and every time I get my blood tested my iron levels are perfect!), but this is an absolutely beautiful fragrant dish that I first had when introduced by a good friend who also happened to be a Head Chef of one of Dubai's best Thai restaurants at the time! Full of amazing goodness!

INGREDIENTS

80g Stir frying beef, very thinly sliced

10ml Olive oil

40g Edamame beans

70g tenderstem broccoli

125ml light Coconut milk

20g Panang red curry paste (or Thai red curry works too!)

1 small white onion, peeled and sliced finely

½ red bell pepper, sliced

2 Kaffir lime leaves

1 teaspoon Fish sauce

1 Red chilli pepper, deseeded and thinly sliced

10g fresh, grated ginger (or Galangal for a more authentic flavour)

1 Garlic clove, grated

1 teaspoon Soy sauce

75g rice, uncooked (I prefer a wild and basmati mixed rice for this)

INSTRUCTIONS

Cook your rice according to the instructions.

Heat a pan on a high heat with the oil and fry your beef. The pan needs to be hot here otherwise you don't cook the beef quick enough and it will go chewy!

Once browned add the Panang curry paste and stir fry for 30 secs, stirring all the time so as not to burn it. Turn the heat to medium and add the onions, broccoli, peppers, garlic, ginger, chilli pepper, kaffir lime leaves, fish sauce and soy sauce. Fry the vegetables until they begin to soften

Add the coconut milk, edamame beans and bring to a boil. Immediately reduce the heat so the coconut milk doesn't split, give it a simmer for 5 minutes, then serve the curry with the rice.

Teriyaki Chicken stir fry with soba noodles

Prepping Time: 10 mins - Cooking Time: 15 mins

I love a stir fry and this one is quick and full of goodness. Did you know peppers are higher in vitamin C than oranges! Great for immunity which helps us runners stop catch the colds! Mushrooms are a powerhouse for immunity too!

INGREDIENTS

100g Chicken breast fillet, thinly sliced

½ each red pepper, green pepper, yellow pepper, deseeded and thinly sliced

20g kale, chopped finely

100g shitake mushrooms, thinly sliced

75g soba noodles (most regular supermarkets sell these)

30g Spring onion, finely diced

10ml olive oil

5ml Sesame oil

1 tablespoon Teriyaki marinade, shop bought

5g sesame seeds

20g toasted cashew nuts to garnish

INSTRUCTIONS

Cook the noodles according to the instructions on the packet.

Marinade your chicken in the Teriyaki marinade overnight.

First, fry your mushrooms in a hot pan with the olive oil; once starting to caramelize, add in the chicken with all of the excess marinades and fry until it is beginning to turn golden.

Add in all the sliced peppers and kale, and cook for a further 2-3 mins until the kale is tender

Add in the sesame oil, spring onions, and noodles, give it all a mix together, and serve with the sesame seeds and cashew nuts sprinkled on top!

Ramen bowl with chicken

Prepping Time: 10 mins - Cooking Time: 20 mins

The food of the running Gods!! This dish has everything, and I know several top ultramarathon runners that devour noodles/ramens during their races! Protein, carbs and the addition of broth make this a bowl of sheer taste, goodness and hydration!

INGREDIENTS

100g Chicken breast, thinly sliced.

1 egg, soft boiled, peeled and sliced in half.

50g White cabbage, very thinly shredded.

30g beansprouts

1 nest of medium egg noodles

25ml Soy sauce

5g Sesame seeds

10ml olive oil

1 Garlic clove, pressed.

10g Ginger fresh and grated.

½ teaspoon Ground coriander

1 teaspoon rice wine vinegar

Pinch of dried Chilli flakes

Handful chopped fresh coriander

3 Radishes, thinly sliced

1 Chicken Stock cube (ideally, you can use a high quality bone broth)

300ml Boiling Water

INSTRUCTIONS

Cook the noodles according to the instructions on the packet but take them out 1 minute earlier otherwise they will go too soft in the broth later!

Desolve the stock cube in the hot water to make the broth.

Heat a frying pan over a medium heat and fry the chicken in the olive oil until it starts to brown. Add in the cabbage, garlic, ginger, ground coriander, chilli seeds, rice vinegar and soy sauce and stir-fry until the cabbage begins to wilt.

Add the cooked noodles to the bottom of a ramen bowl and place the chicken mixture on top. Pour over the broth and top with the boiled egg, spring onions, radishes, sprinkle of sesame seeds and more chilli flakes if you want some extra heat!

Heaven in a bowl!

Beetroot Pesto Pasta

Prepping Time: 10 mins - Cooking Time: 15 mins

Simple, but amazingly delicious! Again, the nitrate power of the beetroots comes in to help us runners here and it's a vibrant dish to have during your carb loading days leading up to a race!

INGREDIENTS

For the pesto:

2 cooked beetroots, drained of any liquid (do not use vinegared beetroots!)

1 garlic clove

30g Pine Nuts, toasted

15g tahini paste

30g parmesan cheese, grated

20ml extra virgin olive oil

6 Fresh Basil Leaves

Pasta:

80g wholewheat spaghetti pasta, uncooked

80g frozen garden peas

20g feta cheese

Handful chopped fresh parsley and basil leaves (and chopped almonds if you like!)

INSTRUCTIONS

Cook the pasta as per the instructions of the packet and add in the peas to the boiling water 4 minutes prior to the pasta finishing being cooked.

Put all the pesto ingredients in a blender until a paste consistency is formed.

Stir the pesto through the drained, warm pasta and serve with feta crumbled on top and the chopped herbs! Stunning!

Any remaining pesto, you can keep in the fridge and serve on toasted sourdough another day or use again for the pasta!

Indian Red Lentil and Cauliflower Dal

Prepping Time: 10 mins - Cooking Time: 25 mins

Get that spice cupboard stocked up!! The health boosting properties in this vegan dish are just phenomenal! With all the incredible spices, lentils and vegetables, this is a great dish for adding nutritious food into your body after a hard run!

INGREDIENTS

100g Cauliflower, cut into small florets

1 teaspoon Virgin Coconut oil

1 medium white onion, diced

90g Red lentils, uncooked

½ can Chopped tomatoes

½ teaspoon ground Cumin powder

½ teaspoon Ground coriander powder

½ teaspoon Turmeric powder

1 tablespoon Medium Curry powder

1 Green chilli, deseeded and finely diced

½ teaspoon Mustard seeds

5g grated fresh ginger

1 clove garlic, crushed and finely chopped

Handful chopped fresh coriander leaves

40g Basmati Rice, uncooked

INSTRUCTIONS

Preheat the oven to 200 °C. Add the cauliflower to a baking dish, and mix together with some salt, black pepper, and the turmeric. Roast in the oven for approx. 20 mins or until you just start to see light browning on the cauliflower

Get the rice cooking as per the packet instructions

Rinse and drain the lentils and add to a pot of water. Bring to the boil, then turn the heat down and gently simmer. Cook until the lentils are tender, which is usually 15-20 minutes.

Heat another large pan over a medium heat and add the coconut oil, onion, garlic, ginger, chilli. Fry until the onions are softened.

Now add the remaining spices and stir well to release the aromas of the spice. After 60 seconds add the tomatoes and cook for 5 minutes

Add the cooked lentils and roasted cauliflower, and simmer over low heat for another 5 minutes. Turn the heat off, add the chopped coriander and immediately serve the dal with the cooked rice! A-MAZ-ING!

Butternut Squash and Bean Bowl

Prepping Time: 10 mins - Cooking Time: 35 mins

INGREDIENTS

1/2 medium butternut squash

1/2 can of black beans, drained and rinsed

100g of sweetcorn, tinned, drained

50g of salsa, shop bought

1/2 ripe avocado, diced

1/2 teaspoon of chili powder

1/2 teaspoon of ground cumin

1/2 teaspoon of dried oregano

1 clove of garlic, minced

Handful of fresh coriander, chopped

Salt and pepper, to taste

INSTRUCTIONS

Preheat your oven to 200°C

Peel the butternut squash and cut it into 2.5cm cubes and place a baking sheet and bake for 25-30 minutes or until the squash is tender and slightly browned.

In a saucepan over medium heat, add in the black beans chili powder, cumin, oregano and minced garlic. Season with salt and pepper to taste. cook the black beans until they are heated through, about 5 minutes.

In a large bowl, mix the roasted butternut squash, black beans, corn and salsa, and avocado.

Serve in bowls, sprinkle with the coriander and enjoy!

Sweet Potato and Chickpea Salad

Prepping Time: 10 mins - Cooking Time: 25 mins

Superfoods galore in the recipe and a good carby salad to top up those glycogen stores!

INGREDIENTS

1 medium sweet potato, peeled and cubed

1/2 can chickpeas, drained and rinsed

50g afresh rocket leaves, rinsed

15ml lemon juice

20ml extra virgin olive oil

1/2 teaspoon ground cumin

1/2 teaspoon smoked paprika

Salt and pepper to taste

INSTRUCTIONS

Preheat your oven to 200°C

Place the cubed sweet potato on a baking sheet and drizzle with 7.5ml of olive oil.

Roast for 20-25 minutes or until the sweet potato is tender and lightly browned.

In a large mixing bowl, combine the roasted sweet potato, chickpeas, and arugula.

In a small bowl, whisk together the lemon juice, remaining 15ml of olive oil, cumin, paprika, salt, and pepper.

Pour the dressing over the sweet potato mixture and toss to evenly coat.

Serve immediately. Enjoy!

Beef-troot Salad!

Prepping Time: 10 mins - Cooking Time: 15 mins

Beef and beetroot bring the red goodness to this gorgeous salad! Protein from the beef to aid in muscle recovery, the complex carbohydrates from the beetroots to replenish energy stores, and the healthy fats and vitamins from the vegetables and cheese

Ingredients:

INGREDIENTS

150g (ish) lean beef steak, grilled and thinly sliced (I prefer sirloin with the fat trimmed off)

2 medium-sized beetroots, roasted and chopped

Good handful of mixed salad leaves (I prefer the peppery rocket and watercress leaves for this salad)

80g cherry tomatoes, halved

1 small chopped red onion

30g crumbled feta cheese

30ml balsamic vinegar

30ml olive oil

Salt and pepper to taste

INSTRUCTIONS

Preheat the oven to 200°C. Wrap the beetroots in foil and roast for 45 minutes or until tender. Let them cool, then peel and chop. Or you could use pre-cooked beetroot

Fry your steak in a very (yes, VERY, this is critical to cooking a perfect steak!) hot pan until it is cooked to your preference (I like medium) and set aside to rest for 4-5 minutes before slicing thinly.

Whisk together the balsamic vinegar, olive oil, salt, and pepper in a small bowl to make the dressing. Arrange the mixed salad leaves on a serving plate and top with the sliced beef, chopped beetroots, cherry tomatoes, red onion, and crumbled feta cheese.

Drizzle the dressing over the salad. Serve and enjoy!

Conclusion

Food plays a crucial role in your overall health and performance as a runner. Food is fuel! By fueling your body with the proper nutrients, you can improve your energy, endurance, and recovery time while reducing the risk of injury and illness.

Remember that nutrition is just one piece of the puzzle regarding running. Complementing your diet with proper training, rest, and recovery is essential to achieve your goals. And if you're ever feeling lost or overwhelmed, don't hesitate to contact a running coach or registered dietitian/nutritionist for guidance and support.

If you want to learn more about nutrition and to run or take your training to the next level, visit my [website](). I support your journey from personalised coaching to resources and tools. Let's get out there and crush those goals!

Afterthought

Congratulations on completing The Ultimate Cookbook for Runners! By now, you should have all the knowledge and resources you need to fuel your body for optimal performance and endurance. Remember, healthy eating is a journey, not a destination. Use the tips and recipes in this book as a starting point, and continue to explore and experiment with new foods and flavors to find what works best for you.

As you continue on your running journey, remember to prioritize your health and listen to your body. Proper nutrition is just one piece of the puzzle, but it's an important one. By fueling your body with the right foods, you can improve your performance, speed up your recovery time, and become a stronger, faster, and healthier version of yourself.

Thank you for choosing The Ultimate Cookbook for Runners as your kitchen companion. We wish you all the best on your running and nutrition journey!

If you enjoyed The Ultimate Cookbook for Runners and found it helpful in your running and nutrition journey, we would greatly appreciate it if you could take a few moments to leave a review on Amazon. Your feedback is incredibly valuable to us and helps other runners find and benefit from this book.

Printed in Great Britain
by Amazon